Unicorn's Hat

'Unicorn's Hat'
An original concept by Amanda Brandon
© Amanda Brandon 2023

Illustrated by Kristen Humphrey

Published by MAVERICK ARTS PUBLISHING LTD
Studio 11, City Business Centre, 6 Brighton Road,
Horsham, West Sussex, RH13 5BB
© Maverick Arts Publishing Limited February 2023
+44 (0)1403 256941

A CIP catalogue record for this book is available at the British Library.

ISBN 978-1-84886-937-0

www.maverickbooks.co.uk

This book is rated as: Blue Band (Guided Reading)
It follows the requirements for Phase 4 phonics.
Most words are decodable, and any non-decodable words are familiar,
supported by the context and/or represented in the artwork.

Unicorn's Hat

By **Amanda Brandon**

Illustrated by **Kristen Humphrey**

"I need a hat," Unicorn said.

He put on a cloth hat, but...

...his horn made a big hole.

He put on a farmer's cap, but...

...his horn spun it too high.

He put on a woollen hat
again and again, until...

...his horn made lots and lots of holes!

"Hats are not made for unicorns,"

Unicorn snorted.

He trotted to a road with diggers and trucks.

He galloped in and out
of the cones.

He said, "A unicorn hat needs to be high, not flat. A unicorn needs a hat like...

...THAT!"

He grabbed a cone and put it on.

"This hat is fantastic!"

The rest of the animals grinned.

"That's not a hat!" they said.

Unicorn hid. He was sad.

Hats were not made for unicorns.

A princess was on a picnic.

She spotted what happened.

"Look!" she said. "I have just the thing."

Then she put her pointed hat on Unicorn and fixed long ribbons to it.

"Thank you!" Unicorn said.

He galloped off.

The ribbons swished in the wind.

Unicorn grinned and said,

"Yippee! This is just right."

The rest of the animals agreed.

"Now that's a unicorn hat!"

they yelled.

Quiz

1. What happened to the farmer's cap?
a) It got a hole in it
b) It was spun too high
c) It got blown away

2. What happened to the woollen hat?
a) It got lots and lots of holes
b) It got one big hole
c) It fell off

3. What did Unicorn gallop in and out of?
a) Trees
b) Signs
c) Cones

4. What did the other animals say about the cone?
a) It was not a hat
b) It was too orange
c) It was too big

5. Who helped Unicorn find the perfect hat?
a) A princess
b) A builder
c) A rabbit

Book Bands for Guided Reading

The Institute of Education book banding system is a scale of colours that reflects the various levels of reading difficulty. The bands are assigned by taking into account the content, the language style, the layout and phonics. Word, phrase and sentence level work is also taken into consideration.

Maverick Early Readers are a bright, attractive range of books covering the pink to white bands. All of these books have been book banded for guided reading to the industry standard and edited by a leading educational consultant.

To view the whole Maverick Readers scheme, visit our website at
www.maverickearlyreaders.com

Or scan the QR code above to view our scheme instantly!

Quiz Answers: 1b, 2a, 3c, 4a, 5a